Advertising & Psychology

The Perfect Duo

The Subliminal Hidden Message

Morgan Grey

ThemeWorks®
Production and Trading

Publication Date:

May 09, 2018

Related Categories:

BISAC: Advertising & Psychology

Binding Type:

US Trade Paper

Trim Size:

5" x 8"

Language:

English

Color:

Black and White

Related Categories:

Cognitive Biases

"Good advertising does not just circulate information. It penetrates the public mind with desires and belief."

— William Bernbach

Contents

Chapter 1 – Overview: Psychology Of Advertising

Chapter 2 –Advertising & Psychology: Understanding The Link

Chapter 3 – What Is The Psychology of Salesmanship?

Chapter 4 – Learn The Psychology of Colors

Chapter 5 – Advertising Yourself As A Brand

Chapter 6 – Decoding The Subliminal Messages

Chapter 7 – Attracting Your Targeted Customers

Chapter 8 – Your Key To Success Advertising "Truth"

Chapter 1 – Overview: Psychology of Advertising

When we speak and discuss about the Psychology of Advertising, the different variety of perception is definitely paramount. After all, your advertisements are all about perception because it is subjective to a certain degree, so you must make the most of each and every advertisement.

You need to know fairly well and in time, *inside out,* what works and what does not, so that you don't waste any time and money on a bad copy.

Long ago, a series of experiments were carried out to determine whether black or white type made a more attractive display for an advertisement. Over five hundred people participated in this experiment.

The white type's background was gray in some cases, but in most cases it was just black. At the end, the results showed that an ordinary reader is more likely to notice a display type in black, than a display type of the same sort in white.

Then, there was another interesting series of lab experiments that was created on the same subject. Specially prepared pages were shown for 1/6 of a second. There were black letters on part of the sheets on white background and white letters on black background.

In the other case, one half of the sheet had words in white type on black background, and the other half had white background containing words in black type.

The scores of cards were then constructed in a way whereby all possible combinations of black and white were made. It was then shown to a handful of persons for such a short span of time, that no one could perceive all there was on any sheet at all.

Under these circumstances, the subjects simply saw what first attracted their attention and also what was easiest to perceive. Later on, the final results showed that the black letters on a white background were seen oftener indeed, compared to the white type on a black background.

This also proves true with other colors as well. Dark font color on a light background is almost always noticed more often than a light font color on a dark background.

You must learn to use the "right combination" unless you are seeking a specific "vibe" for your advertisement.

It seems certain that other things being equal, advertisements will be most often read when printed in type that is the most easily read.

The difference in the appearance of the type in many cases may be so tiny that even the person who is experienced in the choosing of type may not be able to differentiate which ones is more legible, *and yet,* the difference in their values and perceptions of it may be so great that it would be of prioritized importance to the advertiser as to *which* specific type he shall use at the end of the day.

If the matter of the type is so important to the advertiser, then naturally, it is even more important that he makes an extremely wise and careful use of graphics.

So basically, graphics are frequently used mainly as a means of attracting attention but its function to be symbolic is sometimes disregarded for many different reasons.

In a few cases, this may be even necessary, but when we do consider the value of a graphic as a symbol, we are quite taken aback and surprised that graphics are not being used more extensively and judiciously.

The very first form of writing was actually "picture writing" and this was the most direct form and simplest of graphic representation as it is through the pictures and not through the printed words.

At a single glance quickly, we can usually read about four words or so. That is to say, that the width of perception for printed words is about four.

And then at a single glance at the illustration, we can see as much as could be told, in the entire page of printed matter. Thus, we know that the width of perception for illustrations is much more extensive than it is, compared to the printed forms of expression.

It may perform either one or both of two functions: It may be a mere regular picture that is used to attract attention, or it may just simply be an "illustration" and a real help to the perception by assisting the text to tell the story ready to be presented.

In the first case, it would be called an "irrelevant illustration" and in the second case, it is considered relevant. There have been several tests carried on to continue determining the relative attention value of the various relevant and irrelevant illustrations.

Although the results are not as decisive as it might been desired, it seems quite certain that the attention value of relevant illustrations is much greater and that the "irrelevant picture" is frequently not as potent in attracting attention.

Under these circumstances, the illustration in an advertisement should serve as double the function of attracting both the attention and assisting perception. When these two functions can be united in the same illustration, its value would ultimately be enhanced twofold without question.

Generally, irrelevant illustrations are produced because they are there to attract attention, when in reality they may attract the attention of *no one* except the person who have designed them or of the unfortunate person who paid for the service.

Similarly, there are many of these that was produced in advertisements because they are there to assist the perception. They carry an important role of narrating the story of the product advertised, and also to be a form of argumentation.

The designer who is familiar with the goods knows exactly what the picture stands for, so for him, it is a symbol of the product and hence, tells the story of the special advantages.

To the one who is unacquainted with the illustration and with goods that were advertised, the illustration is actually *no illustration at all.*

Not only that, but in many cases, an illustration may actually distract the viewer from the real intended message. Things like the animated graphics may actually draw the eyes away which means the viewer will never get back to the actual message.

The advertiser knows his own product inside out and with what he has to offer that he is often "blinded" by the difficulty the public has in getting a clear and complete perception, by the means of his methods of producing these advertisements.

To the advertiser, you can say that it is almost impossible to err on the side of clearness because he is so familiar with it that he can't imagine otherwise anymore.

On the other hand, a sketchy illustration may appear to be artistic to the designer, but there is always the danger in that it will be regarded as some "meaningless doodle" by the viewer, so you can almost be sure that it will *not* be receiving a second thought or glance from them.

Overall, in conclusion, both the text and illustration should always be crystal clear and it must in every possible way assist and guide the mind of the potential customer in forming the accurate idea of the goods that is being exploited.

This is basically the fundamental rule of what the Psychology of Advertising is all about:

Getting the viewer to remember your product trigger the right emotions (to impress upon them the idea, concept, fantasy or opportunity, to desire and hanker for it) and then proceeding to make a purchase with you.

Chapter 2 – Advertising & Psychology: Understanding The Link

Do you believe that you need a psychology degree to be a good advertiser? Surprisingly, a lot of people actually think so. An advertising journal that dates as far back as 1895 contained an editorial that stated: "When we are a little more enlightened, the advertisement copywriter will study psychology."

It is imperative for advertisers to know the human mind is so that they could have the power to influence it. It's been over a hundred years, and unfortunately, psychology is still not an advertising requirement, yet most advertising modules does include psychological aspects.

Boiling down to the basics, advertising is fundamentally *consumer manipulation.* At times, the manipulation is subtle and other times it's just downright blatant.

But the end result is always the same: sending a message that attempts to influence your behavior by using the "right imagery" to appeal to us on many different emotional levels. Mental imagery plays a massive roll in advertising especially when it comes to newspaper and radio ads.

However, it can be argued that television ads do have an unfair advantage over other mediums simply because moving pictures are often much more effective than still imagery or worse, *no pictures at all.* The colors are brighter, and many of the characters are much easier to relate to, with interesting sounds complementing images and also, all the settings are more diverse.

The newspaper and radio advertising on the other hand, are so much more limited compared to tv ads and hence, the advertisers have to work a lot harder in order to be effective and make a successful advertisement for their product or services.

Advertising can be compared to the human nervous system as our nervous systems also allow us to fully sense the world around us, just like advertisements. We can see, hear, smell, and feel.

Basically, advertising needs to serve the same purpose. It needs to enable us to see, hear, smell and feel the products by creative ways of powerful mental imagery.

Just think of restaurant ads. What "tricks" and "mind hacks" do they use often to make you drop everything and head on over to the diners for a small bite to snack on because you can feel your tongues salivating uncontrollably?

They sell you the "sizzle" as the "meat" of the message, and not the main steak itself, *don't they?*

They know very well that you can't really *smell* the food cooking on the screen, but they sure know that an image of a perfectly juicy steak *sizzling* on a grill will make your mouth water as you remember the smell. It triggers a memory that you remember so well.

On top of that, they'd make sure that the colors are always sharp, because nothing spoils or ruin an appetite quite like a limp tomato garnish and grey gristles. If they are going to use people in the ads, they're *never* so good looking as to be out of reach and it will transport you right away to join them for a meal without feeling out of place.

They will fit you right in, there and then. Pretty amazing, isn't it?

You probably don't even consciously realized you're being sold to. But its happening everywhere and anywhere you go, with ads popping up on your napkins, subways, billboards, influencing each and every one of our choices every single day.

Radio (audio) is also a great medium, because strangely, you don't actually need to see the real food itself to be able *to imagine* how delicious it tastes. All you really need is the sound of the "sizzle" paired with a very strong script.

A strong script is definitely the key if you wish to stimulate strong memories and desires. As you already know by heart, steaks are basically thick and juicy, and your chicken is succulent and tender.

Words can be *just as powerful* as creating imagery and invoking emotions, which is why you must never settle for an "average" script that someone can just "wing it" with such *mediocre* content.

If you are not able to make your audience feel the sun kissing their skins, smell the salty sea entering their lungs and hear the waves ringing in their ear drums, how on earth do you expect yourself to be selling summer vacations?

Psychology can certainly help advertisers learn that certain effects lead to certain reactions which they can effectively use them achieve their ultimate goals and aims. Curiosity is a also an extremely strong motivator to arouse emotions.

If you are able to make your audience curious, you can then easily get them *hooked* and they'll surely proceed to *find out more.*

Psychology may *not be a compulsory* part of the advertising curriculum in all the national schools and colleges, but without the knowledge of what makes people tick, you won't be able to put two and two together.

You would come to find out later soon enough that you can't apply the technical theories of advertising and designs in the real world and get the ROI you deserve on your creative efforts which would definitely make the job *that much more difficult.*

Basically, you got to be (or have) the designer and the salesman as "a package" in order to get the partnership of *both* the advertising and psychology aspect in this creative business.

Say, if you are a designer who *don't know* how to sell, you won't make money from your work. Or.. If you are a salesman *without something* to sell, it would be pointless as well.

But luckily, you can hire (or partner up) with your weakness and fill in the "void" for the things you can't do. But in order to do that, you'll still have to understand the relationship in order to know who to pick for the job that would match up with *your strength.*

Chapter 3 – What Is The Psychology of Salesmanship?

In the very early years, the mention of the word ***"psychology"*** in connection with business was often received with a shrug of the shoulders, raising of the eyebrows or simply a quick change of the subject.

Psychology was a subject was thought to be somehow concerned with the abnormal phenomena which is generally classified as *"psychic" or metaphysical.*

Hence, the average business person impatiently resents the introduction into business speculation with or with "theories and tales" regarding telepathy, clairvoyance, or general spookiness to do with what the eyes can't see *(like our minds and thoughts)*

For these were the things included in his concept of "psychology" back then before there was more education and research on this subject.

But there came a change to the people in business in the later modern years as we evolve and progress into advancement of studies and experiments. They started to hear a lot regarding psychology in business affairs, and started to read a considerable amount on the subject.

They understand now, that psychology means "the science of the mind" and is not necessarily the same subject as the *metaphysics or "psychic."* They started to bring home with them the fact that psychology plays one of the most important part in their business, and that it is worth their time and energy to acquaint themselves with its fundamental principles.

In fact, if they have actually put their open minds and heart sufficiently on the subject, they will have seen that the whole process of selling goods and products, personally, or by means of advertising or display, is essentially a mental process.

Depending upon the state of the mind induced in the consumer, these states of mind are induced solely by the reason of the established principles of psychology.

Whether it's the sales persons or advertisers, they are constantly having to employ psychological principles in order to attract the attention, arouse the interest, create the desire, and moving "the will" of the consumer of their products and services.

The idea of the important part played in business by psychology is one of the most important keys to success in sales of anything.

As applicable it is to personal salesmanship as it is to salesmanship through advertisements: The same principles are always present and consistently operative in both cases.

Chapter 4 – Learn The Psychology of Colors

Did you know that the psychology of color is still within the realms of commonsense and psychology has always been associated with culture?

The significance of color could also be related to particular emotions and situations as well, although there are very few scientific experiments on color or a *"stamped and approved"* color psychology test.

The studies on the effects of colors are mainly on human feelings and behavior and it is believed that red makes people fervent and happy, white signifies purity and cleanliness, while yellow raises alertness, and black evokes a sense of mystery, anonymity or even loss.

Some of the earlier theories of color and its link with psychology could be traced back to the time where it was suggested colors tend to produce high emotional states.

For example, blue produces tranquility and red can arouse emotional states and this all means that they all have certain degree of moral associations.

This is one of the reasons why "Color theory" and the impact of colors have been recognized more than ever before and readily applied in all facets of life right up from all kinds of advertisements down to the interior designs of many beautiful homes and places of interests to not only attract, but also give people a sense of positive emotions that we now know, can be easily influenced with careful planning using the right choice of colors for any types of designs.

Colors that are generally abundant in nature such as green, blue, and brown have much greater resonance as blue being the color of the skies, or perceived as colors of the water bodies seems to create a soothing protective effect. Hence, people naturally associate blue with tranquility, calmness, and serenity.

On the other hand, Green is the natural color of leaves and plants in general, so it symbolizes new life, change, and personal growth. Thus this color is also very well received and accepted because it is recognized as a positive color.

Brown is considered a neutral color because it can be categorized as a *"dull and dark shade"* but it does represent earthiness, wholesomeness, and profound depth because it is closely related to the natural color of the soil *(mother earth)* which gives life to the new seeds.

Generally, natural colors are universal simply because of the familiarity with them having it in our experience daily everywhere we go. Hence, this concept of color resonance could well be used in most of the advertisements or products to represent "au natural" things like "organic" items or highlighting the "freshness" of it.

As for the use of colors in practical life, psychology will have to study the impact of colors in humans more scientifically with a system. There are however, some experiments that relate perception to vision although the main processes are:

▪ Association

As measured with preference for different colors to represent specific situations or events

▪ Attention

As measured with a specific reaction time when a particular color is seen

▪ Retention

As measured with prediction using memory to define particular attributes of the colors

While the properties of color comprising of hues, brightness, and saturation tend to affect reaction time because strong colors like yellow and red can easily evoke the fastest reaction times and they are generally "attention-grabbing colors".

We are often attracted to red, yellow and orange very quickly, although the association of particular colors with specific events can lead to general preference for such colors. Red is also preferred as an emergency color for warnings and dangers in ambulances and fire services, and using any other color will always fail to produce a similar association.

White is actually a very strong color but may not be "attention seeking" during the day. Therefore, color perception is not only dependent on attention drawing properties but also factoring in the association of colors with specific attributes due to cultural knowledge.

This can evoke a lot of human emotions although the emotional aspect of color psychology should require a whole other different kind of study that is more in-depth and thorough, because there is so much more to learn and understand with things we *can only "feel"* but can't always see with our naked eye. Feelings are one of them.

Retention is probably the last phase of color perception which in turn evokes reactions. As from our memory storage, we often predict that specific colors have specific associative properties and they represent certain established concepts.

So in our modern world, red would represent love *(or passion)*, blue would mean tranquility, and white would always represent peace or purity. That is a universal "color language" *everybody* knows.

The psychology of colors have two distinct branches

1. The effects on human emotions with colors - the cultural aspects and emotions of color psychology showing significance in evoking emotions.

2. The effects on perception and human cognition with colors - the physiological and biological reactions involving the phases of association, attention, and last but not least, retention.

Both of these effects of colors will definitely have to be integrated in psychology to truly understand the real significance in shaping our human reactions, emotions, actions, and thoughts.

Hence, these two significant branches of color psychology should certainly be included not just as a theoretical framework in the studies colors psychology but also as a practical framework for applying it into products and services in advertisements.

We are living in the times where visual mediums have attained much significance with the advertisements of various products and messages featured on the world-wide-web, newspapers, televisions, and billboards.

The visual stimuli is an important modern life aspect as we are served with so much visual information and thus, the role of color would be central in our visual experience.

Color psychology should be scientifically studied comprehensively and then applied to all human enterprises, which of course would include education and businesses.

Both branches of color psychology that is dealing with emotions, cognition, and perception will have to be made compulsory in order to fully understand the physiological, cognitive social, cultural, and emotional multi-dimensions of the psychology of color.

Chapter 5 - Advertising Yourself As A Brand

In this digital age, Internet is such a powerful medium of promoting one's brand (and one's self), that there are so many factors to be considered before starting your advertising campaign online, or even offline.

You must above everything else, be very professional in the way your brand's advertising is set up properly in the messages you plan on delivering about your products or services.

More often than not, people's general first impressions of your brand are based on their very first gut reaction to the overall visual impact, and then followed by the text message of your advertising.

So in this case, you really need to be certain that it presents and conveys the most accurate information about you, and *not just that*, but also done *tastefully* in the most flattering manner.

Flattering however, does not mean fabricating lies that are far from the truth. It is remarkable just how quickly word gets out and around if you make false and extravagant claims about yourself or your product. Integrity is the real keynote to follow along with the right values.

This goes without saying that the usage of all grammar and spelling used must be impeccable. Your selection of text styles, fonts, and colors must be balanced harmoniously with caution in order to maximize the potential and effectiveness of any of your advertising.

Your advertisement should have a crystal clear and urgent call to action. This would involve the persuasion to perform a specific desired action on your advertising tool, be it a simple text link or banner.

If the advertising is promoted offline, it will include call-of-actions such as posting cards, picking up the phone, or filling out a coupon. Basically, whether it is online or offline, the desired outcome and needs to fulfill are the same.

Your brand image have to leave the potential customer feeling like they trust you enough to be confident in taking the any of the actions you have dictated. Especially when it comes to a "newbie" trying to establish their own personal branding, the most important key is: *simplicity.*

In most cases, your advertising will only have *a few miniscule seconds* to make its full impact on the viewer.. *Particularly online*, you would only get that split seconds chance to imprint your brand amongst the sea of other brands to make one attempt to dive right into their consciousness.

In such circumstances, usually a well-planned-out design brand logo can be an extremely valuable asset that conveys your message. It would be recognizable when your viewer spots it anywhere else. Next, "power words" that are attention-grabbing or evokes an emotional response are just as important, if not more, in attaching *"your brand image"* to something that your potential consumers would feel positively and strongly about to push them into action.

You got to put the emphasis on the benefits of your brand and not go on endlessly about its features. This is vital and a very important lesson to understand. To further explain, a precise definition, or a "feature", is an aspect of a service that you would be offering.

A "benefit", however, would be the *actual impact* it has on your customer. For example: How is it going to fulfill their aching need or ease their pain and solve the nasty problem?

How is it going to make them feel better about the thing that is causing them so much inconvenience or grief over the years?

You will come to find that it is much more effective to educate your potential customers about the benefits of your brand rather than the features because the market research tests have confirmed this over and over again.

So yes, *testing* advertising strategies is also another vital part of any successful marketing campaigns. First of all, try using a variation of different styles in your initial landing pages for websites along with a combination of different messages mixed and matched up.

Test it patiently by changing one variable at a time until you hit the "jackpot" or "homerun" with the right combination. In other words, *having conversions on it.*

A disclaimer: This specific painstaking step involves a whole series of experimentation, having to collect data from users via tracking system or surveys and having to improve your strategies incrementally and progressively, and there's really no short cuts here whichever way you turn, it still always comes back to this. You can't ever skip this step.

As a testing ground and example, the pay-per-click on Google's AdWords are considered relatively hard to beat *(but not impossible!)* and you have to be very careful in the way you budget your campaigns.

You would have to run each advertisement for a specific frame of time or up to a specific budget. At which point, you would "pull the plug" and cut the campaign dead.

Collect and analyze the response data, fine tune and repeat, until you have "discovered" the right keywords that motivates your niche and also the message *(power words)* that your viewers are responding to.

Always try and incorporate the ultimate power word "Free" in your marketing tests which in most cases would work well depending on the context and the way you frame things.

This is very important as it is often *"the way in"* to gaining your prospect's confidence and then collect their email address successfully if they genuinely feel they have something of value from you at no cost to them.

Making them ask themselves the golden question would be half the battle won when they silently say.. *"What do I have to lose anyway?"*

The psychology of advertising would support this point of view because users may be specifically searching for certain products that are free.

To gain the satisfaction from *your* brand at this point will often put them in a positive state of mind regarding any of their purchases through your system *(mailing list)* in the future.

The other examples would be simply to offer a "free trial" or a "lite version" of a quality software which always gets a good response.

Your customers would find that they really *do want the full version* in the later part after having "a sweet taste" of that *slice of cake* you offered them at no costs first, and then after building "the rapport" and trust, they are much more willing to pay you for the *whole cake* after.

Once that first purchasing commitment to your brand comes through, you have officially cracked the biggest code in building that customer relationship.

Finally, you can proceed to give *even more value* putting more emphasis on the value for money that purchasing your brand can bring to them, making them *recurring* customers.

In summary, always make sure your brand authentically reflects who you are and highlights your values of integrity, honesty, and willingness to go the extra miles to give your best value and services.

As for the choice and medium of advertising devices, just remember to always keep everything crystal clear, consistent and simple, and you have to make sure it is congruent and in tune with the same values your brand advertises.

Finally, last but not least, make 110% sure the products that you offer to someone else solves a real need and would ultimately bring your customers guaranteed satisfaction, and not more frustration.

Start to live up to the image you have created and you simply have to walk the "talk", with the message you have advertised *to the world.*

Chapter 6 – Decoding The Subliminal Messages

Advertising's been one of the longest standing controversial industry where subliminal persuasion has been applied aggressively.

Not surprisingly, the use of this technology became controversial because of questionable ethical usage along with the legal issues involved.

So the national experts have conducted studies on the *real psychological effects* of subliminal advertising to see if it is really effective as it was hyped to be.

Based on the results, there is no doubt that you must definitely look into the use of subliminal messages in advertising because *it will* without question help you dominate your consumer market.

This is exactly what happened with some big branded companies that understood the true power of psychological persuasion and harnessed it.

One of the top brand, Coca Cola, is reported to have experienced dramatic increase in their *"thirst ratings"* after people became exposed to the subliminal messages.

So what different forms of subliminal messages are used in commercials and various other types of ads?

1. Audio

These are songs with subliminal messages embedded in them and some even use songs with messages recorded backward acoustically.

2. Print Ads

The images are hidden in the printed advertisements. They are artistically placed in a position where they can remain hidden but still serves its power and purpose for the subconscious to instantly pick up on.

3. Video Ads

TV commercials also feature images and words that are usually very briefly flashed in matters of split seconds.

Definition of Subliminal Advertising

However, according to the research, the most effective method are having *both the images and words* flashed in between the video scenes and have the subliminal messages embedded in the songs. This combination was found to be a really powerful stimuli which means this technology have proven to hold the ability to affect the psychological state of a person's mind.

The researchers and scientists also found that the psychological effects of subliminal advertising surprisingly were actually quite *temporary,* although very real and powerful.

This is the main reason why if you want subliminal suggestions to be put to test successfully, they have to be applied with repetition until the desired call-of-action is achieved.

Challenges of Subliminal Persuasion

Aside from all these all these useful characteristics of subliminal advertising, there are some warnings that experts wish to add the real definition of subliminal persuasion.

First of all, subliminal suggestions more often than not, works within the bounds of the subject's mind and the characteristics along with the described scenario, and thus, it can trigger very different responses in different individuals.

Since the subject's mind is very limited, marketers have to the take time to widen their perspectives and raise consumer's expectations slowly and surely. Only then, can the subject be more open to dreaming big when it comes in small *incremental doses.*

Apart from that, you simply need to remember to reinforce the messages you want to convey and reach strongly on a very regular basis.

But one of the biggest challenges that advertisers have are the strict rules that some state governments have for the release of advertising materials.

Chapter 7 – Attracting Your Targeted Customers

In today's immense competitive edge in the market, advertisers are constantly trying to introduce *"creative ways"* and means to attract *the right eyeballs*.

As the online business expands exponentially into mainstream, the advertisers would try their best to make the website's presence felt through innovative methods like search engine optimization, link building, and article syndication

Basically, the psychology of behavioral marketing enables the advertiser or website owner to understand the buying behavior of the consumers depending on their activity and movement on the internet.

The website is then fine-tuned and customized in terms of the design, style, navigation, and content to suit the needs of the users and more importantly, attract more potential consumers to the site.

If it was applied to purchase decision, information search, need-based recognition, comparison, or evaluation, you can very easily see a strategy fit for every segment. Marketers must define the principles for using the psychology of behavioral marketing before taking certain risks.

At the root of psychology of behavioral marketing, it is fundamentally an analysis report that is based on learning the behavior to carve out your ideal customer-avatar. This greatly helps to fully understand the purchasing patterns of consumers in a matter of time and targeting the activities of a client that is specially directed not only at one single purchase, but for a lifetime on an annual basis.

As marketers are increasingly trying to comprehend the significance of value for their "lifelong client", they are starting to appreciate the fact that behavioral marketing could be the ultimate source of producing a "re-current" analytical report of consumer trends and patterns.

Once seasoned advertisers who have practiced and mastered the psychology of behavioral marketing, they would instantly 'distinguish' a target visitor as previously visiting the website, and can start to formulate plans to attract and retain that visitor.

Chapter 8 – Your Key To Success
Advertising "Truth"

It seems like in today's world, advertising and business goes hand-in-hand and it's unimaginable to think of one without the other. The brightest minds across America are sitting through their college courses in hopes to graduate for their Associates, Bachelors, Masters, or even PhD's in advertising.

You will see "experts" brainstorming all kinds of ideas in war rooms to come up with the next Ronald McDonald or gecko. Companies would pour out millions of dollars in advertising in the attempt to bring in even more business for themselves.

In the course of having the chance to run my internet ventures and businesses from home in this day and age, I've never intended to spend a dime on another marketing or advertising firm to come up with "gimmicks" to help me sell. I've also never made my intention to misrepresent anything I do just to *"bait and lure"* in business.

However, I planned to be successful from the very start even without "traditional" advertising. You must be wondering... *How?*

Simple. I plan to advertise "Truth" through networking.

Why do you think you automatically set your DVR to skip through all the commercials? Why do you find yourself "channel surfing" for an alternative music station on the radio *as soon as commercials come on*? Let me tell you why. You do it for the exact same reason that virtually every single station goes to commercial at the same time! That is because you and the stations both *know you don't want* to hear any of their "sales pitch".

Just think about it a little deeper, and you will come to realize it all really boils down to the fact that you simply don't trust advertisements *(with good reason I might add).* That is for the same reason your blood pressure rises just a little more when confronted a used car salesman, or worse, someone trying to sell you an insurance *for life.* You just simply *don't trust* them.

In my humble opinion, this concrete "wall of mistrust" have been directly caused by traditional advertising over the many decades of marketing and sales stereotypes instilled in people. Over here, I would like to take the chance to share a couple arguments to support my views.

As you know by now, virtually every strategy in advertising has been wrapped in some level of psychology.

Common Advertising Strategies

Every strategy in essence was fundamentally set up to outsmart consumers and basically manipulate them into buying the product.

Have you ever *wondered why* the bread and milk are always **on opposite ends** of the grocery store when they know very well most people are coming in for *both products*?

Now that is simple psychology. By having them on opposite ends of the store, you'd **have to** walk across all the 8 other lanes where you would be *face-on* confronted with other hundreds more products in between. Chances are.. you will probably pick up something you never intended to when you stepped in.

Why do think car lots offer cars at $19,998 instead of simply saying $20,000?

Again, it is simple psychology. Strangely, twenty thousand sounds *so much more* than a price only two dollars lower. Moreover, now they "technically" can say they are offering the vehicle for under $20k even though you and I know deep down, it is simply not true.

Still not fully convinced, that advertising was geared and designed to manipulate you? Now, I challenge you to watch commercials for popular beer brands tonight. Look out for it and watch it carefully. Personally, I've never open up a beer and have snow bunnies in a hot tub show up. Basically, it's all but subtle mind tricks.

Not only does traditional advertising play mind games with you, it will consistently mislead you in ways that will blow your minds when debunked. Most people really go through their entire lives not knowing *(or choose to deny because it fills them with guilt and shame)* and they would continue on their impulsive splurges and unhealthy ways of consuming products.

Case scenario: Say you're watching TV and a commercial pops on for a satellite provider and it is advertising the unlimited channels you can possibly watch for just $19.99. Meanwhile, along the bottom of the screen is a series of what appears to be fonts that is so tiny, you will probably need cataract surgery, if you even attempt to squint your eyes and focus to read it.

So what do you think the odds are that you will get "actual price" that was quoted so boldly in the advertisement? I can tell you *right now*, it is slim to none. In that series of illegible script, there will be an entire list of other "hidden" charges that are not openly shared in the advertisement.

Technically, it's **not** false advertisement because it was in that block of "Terms & Conditions" as you would normally see in "fine print" but we all know that that is not ethical nor trustworthy. Yet, this is what traditional advertisement as it stands today in a world of "noise" and information-overload.

This is what I truly believe and stand for. Gimmicks and sales always bring in a specific group of "fly-by shoppers" who is *looking for something for nothing*. In other words, the cheap "free-loaders".

However, honesty and trust is the key to building a good rapport with people who are truly looking *for value.* You see companies like Wal-Mart driving down prices as well as lowering quality. Sadly, the same is true in most walks of life.

But there is a simple <u>two-step process</u> to reverse this trend. First of all, be trustworthy *in everything* you do. As old fashioned as it may sound right now, I can't emphasize enough how much people should be able to come to trust you at your word wholeheartedly.

Secondly, you must find a way to provide a top-notch world class product that brings great value to the consumer and provides most of the benefits *(if not all)* that they are looking for.

When you can combine these two key ingredients, you won't even have to lift a finger to advertise, your customers will do all the advertising ***for you.***

They *will start* to spread the word. Ever heard of the power of "word-of-mouth"? So you must be asking, will it take longer? Probably. Will it pay off at the end of the day? Definitely.

The bottom line is this, the everyday advertising right now is "out dated" and *archaic at best*. It's the same melody and rhythm being played by hundreds and thousands of different people.

As I mentioned above, the *best ingredient* in advertising is still.. the "TRUTH". It's the only way these days to build a sustainable and long-termed business. Unless you plan to "hit and run."

Traditional advertising can no longer effectively accomplish this with the overwhelming usage of technology, because anyone can easily "google the truth" in a heartbeat the minute they sense something doesn't add up with the "advertised features".

Networking on the other hand, through *(social media)* sites such as personal blogs on your websites, Facebook, Twitter, or Instagram gives potential customers the opportunity to get to know you personally.

Just imagine how much of an impact you will leave behind as a tangible footprint in their lives and even touch their hearts if you are lucky enough.

I personally have never got the rare chance to ever speak to a company's CEO or president for my "necessity products" I consume, and I don't know any customers who get these kind of chance to do so on a daily basis.

But with a good solid foundation of a proper channel and network, your customers will not only get to know who you are, they can immediately have a **direct-connection** to you. They can easily leave their feedbacks and comment to you personally about the product or service you provide and leave you with plenty of room for improvements and changes.

They will also eventually become more than just your "customers", they might even become associates or a unexpected blossoming friendship. Most of all, you will have one thing that traditional advertising cannot accomplish: Loyalty from your clients.

Why? Simply because .. they trust you.

About Author

Morgan Grey double-majored in Communications Design & Psychology and Masters in Advertising.

Currently he is an Internet marketing specialist and possess extensive knowledge about behavioral marketing and targeting and also had a decade of experience running a Creative Company as Co-founder and Senior Creative Director.

His passion for both advertising and psychology has enabled him to put this simple and no fluff summary of the link between them and also how to apply it in our daily lives, stretching our potential and knowledge to understand it better so that we can make better conscious choices as a consumer or even becoming an expert master advertiser.

"The purpose of psychology is to give us a completely different idea of the things we know best." - P. Valry

Recommended Courses To Use Your New Skills & Knowledge To Make Passive Income

A List Of The Best E-Commerce Internet Marketing Opportunities To Work From Home

Download Free Kindle With Every Paperback Purchase

To Access Links Directly

Ecom Profit Sniper

The AZ CODE

Internet Jetset

Salehoo Dropship Directory

Are You a Non-Fiction Book Junkie?

Access Over 150 Non-Fiction Niches

For Free at Our VIP LibraryBox Today

Yes, I Want To Receive Free Books

In My Favorite Niches

Download Free Kindle With Every Paperback Purchase

To Access Links Directly

Made in the USA
Monee, IL
07 August 2020